MW00562365

MRS. SCHMETTERLING

ARROWSMITH

PRESS

Mrs. Schmetterling
Robin Davidson

ISBN: 978-1-7376156-4-4

Boston — New York — San Francisco — Baghdad
San Juan — Kyiv — Istanbul — Santiago, Chile
Beijing — Paris — London — Cairo — Madrid
Milan — Melbourne — Jerusalem — Darfur

11 Chestnut St.
Medford, MA 02155

arrowsmithpress@gmail.com
www.arrowsmithpress.com

The thirty-ninth Arrowsmith book
was typeset & designed by Ezra Fox
for Askold Melnyczuk & Alex Johnson
in Garamond and Palatino Linotype fonts

MRS. SCHMETTERLING

Poems by Robin Davidson

with artwork by Sarah Fisher

for Ewa Lipska & Carolyn Forché

CONTENTS

Mrs. Schmetterling

MRS. SCHMETTERLING KNEELS IN A GARDEN

Mrs. Schmetterling, let's call her Judith, married.
She is neither great musician nor poet.
Not scientist nor historian. She is ordinary.
Any century's woman. She cooks, reads, bathes children
and dogs. She takes out the garbage, listens to music.
Mrs. Schmetterling is tired. Her imagination is
pressed like a tiny chestnut blossom between the pages
of old letters and recipes, a book of days.
She would like to give herself advice, chide herself
not simply to feed on the erotic bread of great art,
remain invisible. But she doesn't. She hesitates,
keeps herself at arm's length. A practice
she's learned from her mother. Instead,
she kneels in a garden, breaks open
each amaryllis pod in her palm, peels back
the green triangles of skin forming the bolus
left from the blossom and sprinkles
the black ash of seedlings onto the clay.

MRS. SCHMETTERLING THINKS OF HER HEART

Mrs. Schmetterling thinks of herself as a visible whole
not as parts, a conglomeration of molecules.
She is not a scientific woman.
When she thinks of heart, that rocking, flopping in her chest,
she does not see in her mind's eye a muscle
or chambers, or bloody arteries twitching, rather
she sees cranes rising from a marsh *en masse*,
their extended wings, a white blanket of fluttering
that propel her to her feet and then to the mailbox.
She loves letters, or the thought of letters,
and the oceans they have crossed, braiding the world
together like a handful of hair resting along her shoulder.
She is enviable in this way, for she makes all things
rise up from within. Even the most disparate of objects or ideas—
the reading of Wittgenstein's *Tractatus* and schnitzel recipes,
the map-pencil drawings of her childhood
and the hubris of war's vowels, Lwów, Lvov, Lviv—
seem to coalesce within her own warm body,
her own inner life and the world's.

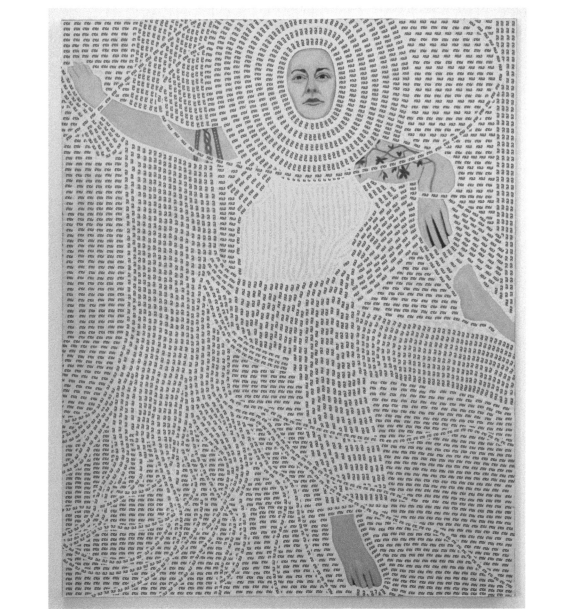

CITY THAT RIPENS ON THE TREE OF THE WORLD

The tree outside Mrs. Schmetterling's flat in a foreign
city is a cathedral. Its black branches are stones,

luminous with ice windows.
The tree's single chorister is a black and white magpie

whose visible grace is a persistent scavenging.
She knows such scavenging.

She loves this bird.
Mrs. Schmetterling watches the November

seasonal seam open to a dual harvest.
She lives at an intersection

where Krupnicza Street crosses Mickiewicz Avenue,
where barley and the great Romantic poet collide.

When night falls, Mrs. Schmetterling will see
two moons rise outside her window,

like laundry hung out piece by piece
over a balcony in winter wind. One pure, bright,

the original moon. The other, its shadow
or some odd reflection caught

on the outside of the glass in the branches. No,
both hang in the inner lace of curtains along her desk,

so that she stands, takes the lace in her hands,
turns it to the left, the right.

But this doubleness stays.
Twin sisters of half-light, side by side,

hovering above her. If only one of them turned,
the moon would be full.

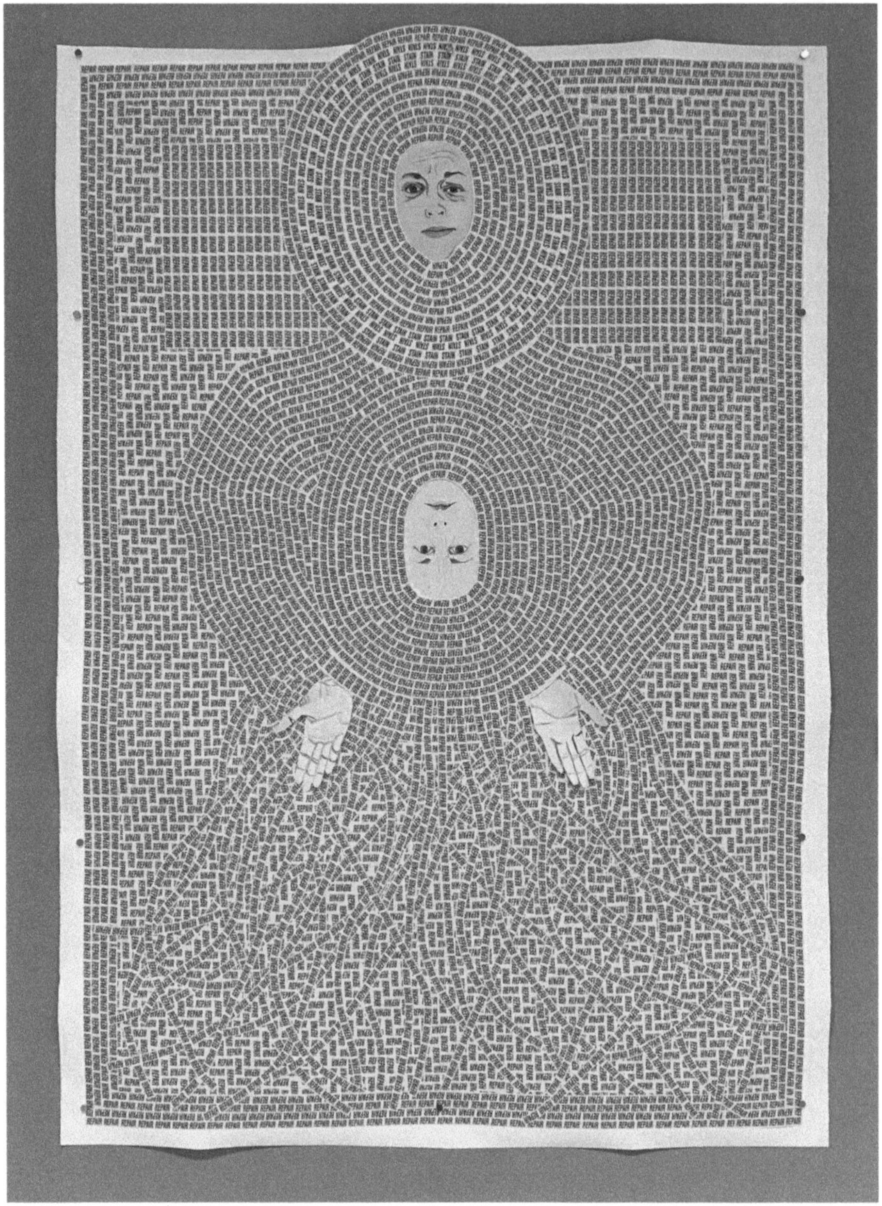
REPAIR
STAIN

MRS. SCHMETTERLING CONSIDERS THE BEAUTIFUL

Mrs. Schmetterling looks on beauty
as an interior landscape, the moonrise of her imagination.
When she closes her eyes, she sees the room's ceiling
fill first with billowing shadows, then a pinpoint of
light that blooms into a blue-black shining, then
the brilliant blue of coronal plasma that could
be the widening eye of God. Or a host of
angels navigating a great abyss, their
wings clapping out light. But Mrs. Schmetterling is
skeptical of the sublime. She does not trust a transcendence
that will come to her on the day the world ends.
She believes in what she can see, hold
in her mind's eye. Cold, hard snow
in muddy clumps melting, kicked aside.
Chestnut trees lining the avenues, their tiny candelabras
of blossom upon blossom, at the bud's edge, waiting.
Ubiquitous sparrows flitting among the branches,
then among tulips when they bloom at last.
The romantic vestige of old musicians
spilling their song into the square.
The other music of boot clicks
on stone. All this she carries
as the roiling blue that rises
like a wall, a tidal wave
of light behind her eyes.

SORITES AND SAND

Mrs. Schmetterling has been thinking about boundaries,
how the borders of countries and of gardens overlap,
how words themselves melt into one another—prefix, suffix, root—
until she is now swept away
in a sea of sentence upon sentence, drowning.
Recently, in her mind's ear, she's begun to confuse
siostry and *sorites, sisters* and *a heap of sand.*
What words she wonders are necessary for sister
syllogisms to build upon each other,
not by heaping but weaving,
like the loom work of a great queen.
Mrs. Schmetterling could build a kingdom
on the threads of a shroud. She could stretch strands
of cowhide wide to build a city.
She could be a woman poised to speak
if these thoughts running wild in her head
could converge, compose the seamless fabric
of a slow-moving river, each syllable,
a rivulet, a warp or weft thread
floated inextricably into each sister stitch,
world to word, word to world.

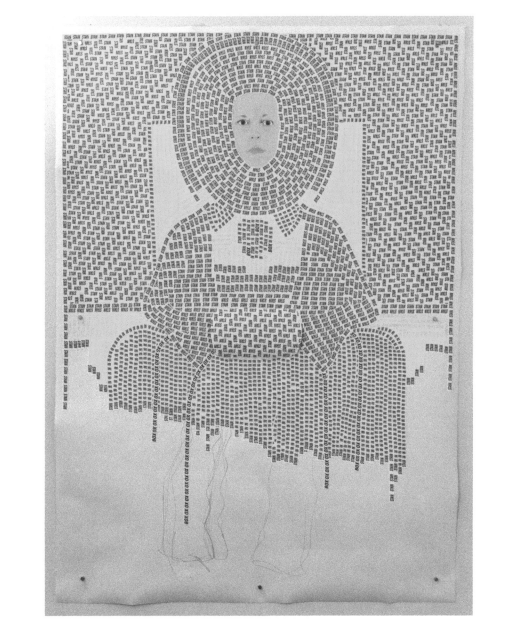

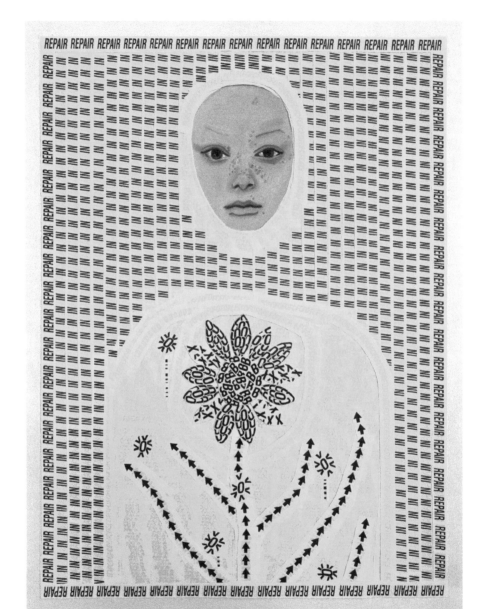

CHESTNUT TREES

The paths of the Planty are lighted by chestnuts,
each tree a candelabra of blossoms,
each blossom a candle of miniatures—

clusters of dolls' orchid corsages
or tiny white labia opening into tongues of pink flame,
a party, a Pentecost, the soul dressed up.

Mrs. Schmetterling knows these trees herald a season:
Late spring, the thief of dolls who leaves desire
in its wake. She remembers the thrill of

longing, opens her ungloved hands to the sky,
and walks unhurried beneath chestnuts,
their blossoms, loosed and floating,

stones skipped across the Planty pond of sky,
holograms of concentric light,
which fall in flakes, iridescent as fish scales or fire.

WHAT MRS. SCHMETTERLING WANTS

Mrs. Schmetterling wants nothing more
than the landscape, the city's opening
onto streets of stones, shops, small wrought iron tables
hung with umbrellas, set with cloth napkins, beer.
She meanders among apartment buildings, window boxes
bursting with petunias, cloud whites, bubble gum pinks,
the purples of bruises, buried blood.
She watches the train station walls blooming with graffiti.
Mrs. Schmetterling does not want history.
She wants the graffiti to color old concrete, cover the blood.
She lives between kitsch and the weight of stones,
the exhibit of painted noses, torsos, giant sunflowers
at the city gate, and the gate itself.
She wants nothing more than her soul's wilderness
taking hold at the city's edge, spreading like milkweed
in the garden plot that no one owns,
no one owns.

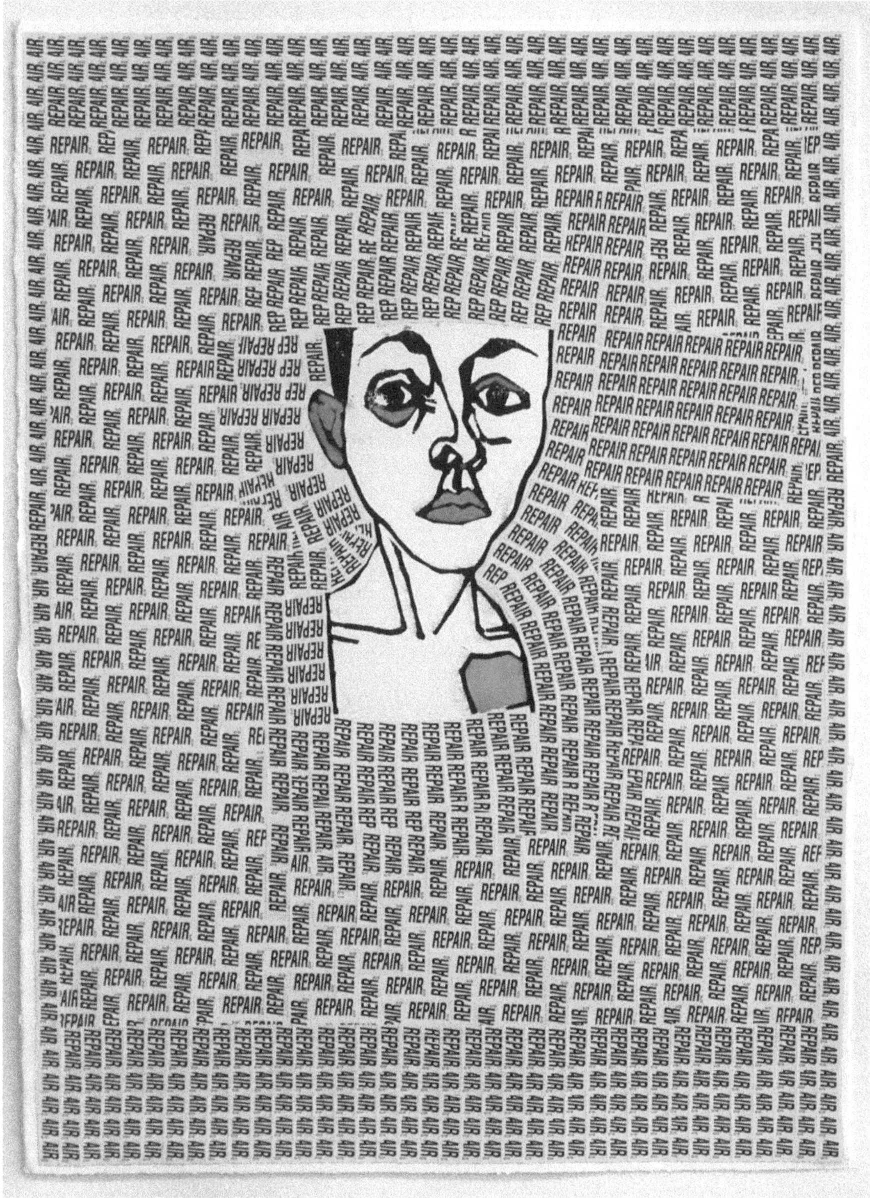
AIR
REPAIR

STAIN

Mrs. Schmetterling hears the Dean of Coventry Cathedral say,
We are all angels. We can all be ambassadors of forgiveness.

The figure on the canvas looks like an angel, or a nun,
until Mrs. Schmetterling sees she's made of tiny, yellow rectangles.

Strips of tape that read, *Stain.*
The figure on the canvas is made of laundry stickers and failures,

one after another, an avalanche of human error.
The Dean says Coventry Cathedral rose from the ruins, rebuilt

with charred beams and marked with the Cross of Nails
to forgive the wounds of history, cleanse the traces.

The figure on the canvas has the face and hands of a woman.
Eve in a habit. Eve with yellow, laundry tape wings.

Mrs. Schmetterling too is an accumulation of stains.
She wonders how she, or anyone, removes the stains of history.

She studies the woman's face, her open palms
for a salvation story, the human sacrifice required of her.

But what she sees is a labyrinthine body of sleeves and wings,
tunic and coif, a weave of wounds and stains

whose beauty shines like a mother-father-god.
Mrs. Schmetterling hears the rhyme of *stain* in *angels*.

She thinks of history as a planetary dry cleaners
where humankind's soiled laundry is sorted and marked,

soaked with solvent or water, and waits for ablution
or ash.

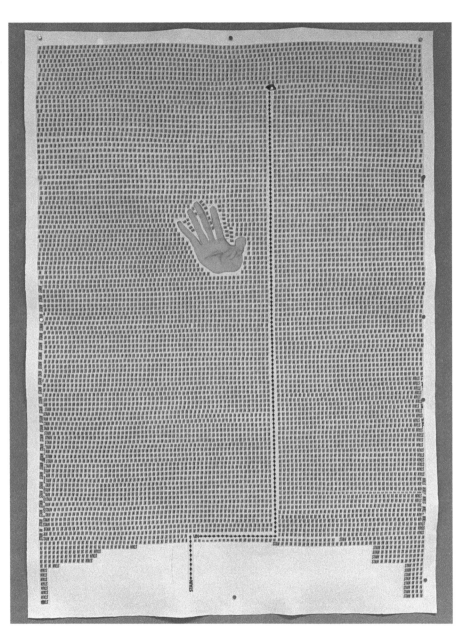

IN THE BALANCE OF FINAL THINGS

Mrs. Schmetterling has been reading *The Egyptian Book*
of the Dead and now when she lies down to sleep
she sees in her mind's eye the balance of final things.
She imagines herself before a tribunal of gods
in human masks. She counts each face like sheep—
old Marx, old Miłosz, one, two. The young Baczyński, three.
Joseph Stalin in a white moustache, baby Adolf in a white smock,
the Black Madonna of Częstochowa, four, five, six.
She sees Europe, east and west, under a sky of fireworks and ash.
She keeps counting, watches the high scales
suspended above her head, one pan drooping
beneath the weight of a single stone.
Mrs. Schmetterling considers her life, waits for the moment
she must place her own heart in the balance.
She wonders what punishment awaits a heart too light.
She regrets laughter, the warmth of her down comforter,
her own fate lucky, random, unearned.

MRS. SCHMETTERLING CONSIDERS THE INVISIBLE

Mrs. Schmetterling has been reading what scientists say
     about theories of cloaking, and now she thinks
          she's beginning to understand her own invisibility.
               She wonders how fast or how slowly light must travel

across her face to hide her eyes, nose, mouth, chin,
     how much time it will take to erase her person entirely.
          Or what if not only she as an object, but her life
               as an event, disappear among particles of racing light.

          At first she tells herself she must wake up,
     break whatever magnetic field she's prisoner to, and be seen.
But Mrs. Schmetterling decides otherwise. She prefers to move through her life,
feeling her way in the dark, along streets and walls, furniture and faces,

          to better see suffering, large and small, the latent text
        of lives shaped in the muscles of a hand, in the deep blue shadows
     beneath the eyes. She must wear invisibility from within,
swallow the light that eludes her until she glows.

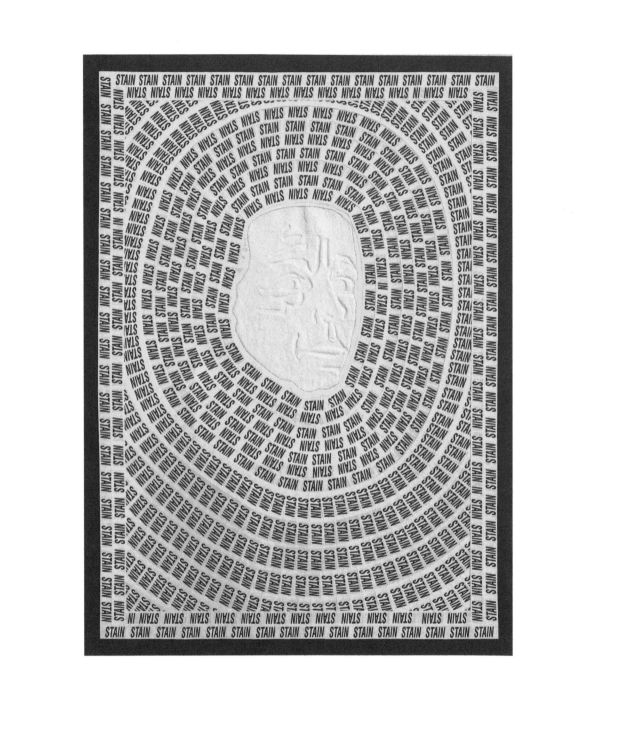

BLINDNESS

The ancient prophets were often blind, and not particularly well received.
Consider Tiresias or Cassandra or Homer himself.
Or Eli or Ahijah the Shilonite, even Paul along the road to Damascus.

Musicians too have been known to be blind. Old bluesmen
like Blind Lemon Jefferson or the Blind Willies—Johnson and Mctell—
or Ray Charles on the keys. Though music may make truth

easier to accept. Mrs. Schmetterling too has begun to lose her sight,
though she hasn't discovered any ancillary prophetic powers.
Mostly she sees the blurred words of can or bottle labels.

The hazy pages of newspapers or long beloved books. The faces
in family photographs too fuzzy to make out who's who. She gathers
reading glasses of all kinds, scatters them like seeds

about the house, scorns the tiny jeweled chain that might keep
a single pair at the ready round her neck. Small rebellion
against encroaching dark. She hasn't yet noticed some inward vision

replacing the disappearance of a world whose shapes, colors she's
found riveting since childhood. She waits patiently for this revelation,
the way December forsythia waits for spring.

Mrs. Schmetterling Buries Her Mother

Mrs. Schmetterling has spent much of her life trying to bury her mother,
but now that she's actually covered her casket with eucalyptus, white roses,
seen her laid deep in the ground, her mother has begun to appear everywhere:
In the way Mrs. Schmetterling opens a package of mint gum, chews it leisurely
at first, then nervously as she rides in the car beside her husband as he drives.
In the most surprising exclamations studiously avoided in her former vocabulary:
For Pete's sake! Whose sake is this? A child's, a neighbor's, the beloved saint's?
In the way her nose detects the smallest waft of household odors,
bursts into sneezing at the faintest manufactured floral scents,
or in the many Kleenex boxes she's begun to place throughout the house,
the previously dismissed tissues appearing like tiny ghosts in her hands, her pockets.
In her morning call to the green anoles weaving themselves among the jasmine
or in the vigil she keeps for hummingbirds, their wingbeats frenetic,
nearly invisible, what a soul-in-miniature must be, passing through the garden.
In the toes of her right foot where one begins to cross the other, an involuntary braiding,
soon to rob her of the smooth-fitting shoes she's loved for years.
In her own face, a familiar curve of mouth or cheekbone she can't disguise
even with the most expensive powders. A face whose crooked half-smile
she misses now, but is returned to her each morning in the mirror.

A WHITE STONE

"To him who overcomes, I will give some of the hidden manna. I will also give him
a white stone with a new name written on it, known only to him who receives it." —Revelation 2:17

She is seeking a new name, not one to be received at death,
but another living name written in the deepest indigo within her chest.

She takes long walks in her neighborhood, scours the grasses
and sidewalks for flat stones that might serendipitously appear in her path

and reveal the traces of an ink she believes only she can see.
Mrs. Schmetterling is not so much superstitious as she is faithful,

believing that any miracle is possible if willed long enough
and seen with precision in the deepest recesses of a skilled imagination.

It's likely this commitment to search among stones
that's made her at home in cemeteries, their miniature houses landscaped

with chrysanthemums and violets, with small brooms
stashed beside low mausoleum doors or the headstones of graves.

She watches whole families sweep away the debris
accumulating among leaves and lighted lanterns, votive candles.

A world of incarnate memory where the living and the dead
meet in a harmonious silence to walk among names carved and gleaming,

a stronghold against erasure until the perfect white stone
appears, illuminates the until-then invisible word she will already know.

MRS. SCHMETTERLING VISITS MONTPARNASSE CEMETERY

She admires the headstones, their script engravings, floral images.
She reads each name and date with care. Whole lives

held beneath the cold but splendid marble.
As she walks along the gravel path among lindens,

she looks for tangible monuments of her century's artists,
what she can touch, hold in her hands. She searches

first for Baudelaire, as well hidden in death as the subtleties
of his verse were in life, those forests of symbols.

Or Robert Desnos, his more lyric French trilling in memory.
She looks for Man Ray but can't find him. She wonders

what love is still buried between him and Lee Miller's
naked bones. She walks until she finds Sartre and de Beauvoir,

their shared headstone covered with kisses, *bien sûr*.
And then the other Simone, her beloved one,

who, like she, waits for God. But Mrs. Schmetterling is not one
to let ambition or mystic grace crowd out living.

She pauses longest before Marguerite Duras, reads love notes
covering the stone, as many as she can until she sees

the open notebooks, lined, unfilled, and pencils, pencils, pencils—
to write unceasingly from the grave. She takes the stub

of pencil from her pocket, places it in the overflowing jar,
kisses the glass, and walks on in the morning sun.

OAK COTTAGE

Mrs. Schmetterling has left home for a forest near
a stratovolcano, to stand on the porch of a cottage built of oak.
The sun rises among cedars in a reddening sky.

She has come here for long walks in silence. No,
she has come here for birdsong, the sound of moving water:
brook-song. That these might enter her blood.

She follows a path through hellebore and ivy to
a fallen tree, a bench of sorts, where she listens for her mind's
voice grown mute in the cadences of city traffic.

Mrs. Schmetterling wants to remember beauty in a
world bereft of grace, to watch fern fronds ripple among grass
in peace, where human presence is subdued by wind,

sea waters, the height of cedars. She wants to release
in the cells of her body a brightness like starlight, not the human
form burning, but a radiance attributable to the gods.

She watches an owl overhead, sees the wingspan
of the great bird as the transcendence she seeks but has not yet
found. She bows her head, waits, as the wings glide

upward. Mrs. Schmetterling knows she is small here,
seated before a pond overgrown with rushes, willow branches,
their fountain of golden limbs. She wades among

these willows in her mind, wanders the smoldering
wilderness within her, listens for the magma of a subterranean
truth, its murmur.

CHILDREN

It's possible they've saved her from the abiding force of ambition
that once moved in her like the pulse
of relentless rain.

It's possible they've crushed her like a lawnflower, unseen
in the *sturm und drang* of colliding bodies, their growing limbs racing
 reckless in the grass.

Mrs. Schmetterling was not prepared for children.
She imagined her life in a forest or desert, listening to silence.
Or on prayerful walks in a cloister of sisters.

Or painting from the Montmartre stone steps at dawn, recreating
the Sacré-Coeur in reds and golds, a carousel of light.
But fate had other ideas.

These days the little tumblers she watches are her children's children.
They run to meet her. One leaps, curls his long legs
around her waist. The other cries

to be held, anchors himself to her collarbone with chubby fingers.
Love is sweat and mud and her old, wild heart
pressed to these jam-smeared faces.

MRS. SCHMETTERLING ON MAGIC

There's a difference between magic and trickery
in the five-year-old mind.

At the musical program for children, "A Curious Christmas,"
a magician holds a deck of playing cards.

He shuffles, cuts the deck, hands a card to each child
sitting in the auditorium's front row.

Miraculously he's able to guess correctly the Queen of Diamonds
the girl with the blue barrette holds tight.

The magician makes two gold coins disappear from his gloved palm
and reappear with a clink in the pail at his feet.

Mrs. Schmetterling's grandson is skeptical. He knows
a trick when he sees one,

but when the program comes to a close, and the great bearded
Santa of myth appears on stage,

his red wool suit and hat gleaming in the theatrical dark,
all the children jump to their feet.

They stand on their chair seats, climb the aisle railings.
They laugh and clap, begin to sing.

Even Mrs. Schmetterling, who's long forgotten all believing,
knows when magic enters a room.

MRS. SCHMETTERLING UNTRIMS THE CHRISTMAS TREE

She considers the scent of the dying tree, an overripe sweetness.
She thinks of the cedars of Lebanon, their divinity corrupted

by human presence—merchant fleets, temples, rolls of papyrus.
Even the Egyptians she's admired stripped the sacred wood of sap

to prepare their dead for passage. She too corrupts the forest.
She holds each ornament carefully in her palms, wraps them in tissue

made of delicate pulp. Each, a small bundle of memory.
She works backward: The silver-framed miniatures of her grandsons,

the wooden Kraków angels, pink and blue, and two glass hearts
in red and gold circumscribed by a baroque braid of Polish ribbon

for her son and daughter. Construction paper self-portraits
her children made, their small faces glowing from each center.

The tree-top star made of pretzels, turned to near stone by time.
The icicles and bells of painted glass, thinning, translucent

from the first season with her young husband. Her own creations
as a child, Santa faces made of buttons, cotton-ball beards,

paper funnel hats glued to each shining globe. The Triestine
bell and mandolin her mother bought before her birth, shipped

across an ocean. Mrs. Schmetterling considers the weight
of the ornaments she holds, how they grow heavier each year,

like objects traveling faster and faster, never reaching light speed
but never quite slowing in the path of past, present, future,

the grammar of living she knows she too will leave one day,
her possessions *waving adieu* and left to others' hands.

Mrs. Schmetterling looks around her dining room.
Her gaze settles on the tabletop, objects she knows by heart

spilling out along the grains of wood, an unraveling she gathers,
packs away, the Christmases accumulating like dust.

LIMBO AT THE EDGE OF AN ABYSS

Mrs. Schmetterling has developed a fever. She reads the morning paper,
watches the evening news, and all she can see are hospital corridors—

a flurry of doctors hovering above supine victims at a hospital in Queens.
The floors lined with men and women huddled on makeshift beds

in Spain. Red Cross hospital tents and ventilators stationed in a parking lot
in northern Italy, where medical staff in hazmat gear tend

those who cough, burn with fever. Mrs. Schmetterling imagines
her own lungs filled with hundreds of tiny crowns, each an empire, warring

for possession of her breath. But she feels no such battle in her chest
beyond the paralysis of her own fear. She props her head against the pillows

and recites the few poems and prayers she can remember from childhood,
not as healing but as distraction from the images of illness that haunt

her when she closes her eyes. She tries to imagine a garden filled
with heather and milkweed. Her hands, sunk in soil, tether her to earth,

to the lilies, cannas, her neighbor's gift of fire bush, while her fever
burns. She begins to see Monarch butterflies circling the ceiling like fan blades.

Mrs. Schmetterling is named for butterflies, and is as fragile. She, like
the world, is restless, waiting for an end to the limbo at the edge of an abyss

she knows exists but is hidden, an unknown she does not know
how to contemplate. She sinks into her pillows and the damp of sweat

along her neck. She's at home, after all, not in a tent or on a cold hospital floor.
She promises herself she will survive. She will no longer live like a stone,

but will break her stillness, rise up: Lupines grown wild among cedars.
A whole meadow opening into sparrows, ascending.

COLOR THEORY

Mrs. Schmetterling loves color. She often wishes she'd been a painter
like her mother. She looks forward to the digital *Color of the Month*

swatches arriving from Sherwin-Williams in her email:
"Coral Clay" is June, preceded by "Wild Poppy," "Storm Warning,"

"Oat Milk," "Featherstone," "Nocturne"—one of the few
pleasures she finds in quarantine.

Mrs. Schmetterling tried taking art classes once, but her days
as an artist were few. Instead, she paints walls.

The bathroom in "Mink." The kitchen in "Accessible Beige."
The dining room in "Tomahawk," a burgundy her mother hated

as reminder of the dreaded piano room of her childhood.
She's tried reading Goethe's theory of color, but she doesn't understand

why *the principal phenomena in chemical colors are produced by oxidation.*
She thinks of oxidation not as a scavenging of electrons, but as a theft

of air, the breath burning. And what about other chemical realities:
Pure water crystalized to snow appears white... Black is not exhibited

in so elementary a state.... She doesn't understand the science of chemical
elements. She'd rather consider Kandinsky, his belief in the spiritual

vibration of colors, the moods and emotions they create—
warmth or cold, harmony or chaos, relief or angst.

She learned as a child to think of color in binaries,
their shades a more precise cataloging of relationships opposed

on the color wheel. She knows now that binaries oversimplify,
but who should have power to complicate a shade, to name a paint

for blood and blame, or purity. Mrs. Schmetterling's skin, her life
have been a kind of white, "Pure White" or "Alabaster,"

or even just "Natural Choice." She believed her face and hands
should be rose clay, oat milk, a touch of wild poppy.

Ah, blind vanity. She grieves.
She holds her paintbrush to the light, and sees

an ugliness that will never stay covered, no matter
how many gallons of paint the world may offer.

Generations of cracks, stains unmasked.
Walls crumbling, revealed as decay.

MRS. SCHMETTERLING THINKS OF RETURNING TO THE CITY WHERE SHE WAS BORN

Mrs. Schmetterling thinks of returning to the port city of her birth
when the pandemic passes.

What will she recognize from her first year of breath in this world?
The scent of sea air? Words in Italian?

She closes her eyes and conjures window boxes of geraniums and phlox
coloring white-washed stucco walls.

She imagines cobblestone streets as narrow as alleyways, and the child
she was, jostled along beneath

the stroller's black canopy, beneath laundry billowing from wrought-iron
balconies, and the great Duomo.

She's standing now, clinging to her mother's hands and descending
an undulation of stone steps into

a piazza, its labyrinth of tiles and bricks, the geometric city spiraling.
She's unsure what she remembers,

and what she's conjured from old photographs, family stories,
or the intermittent longing

for a Europe that calls to her, like a film run and rerun where men
in uniforms glowing with stars stand,

eating gelato, history rising like an ancient chorus that collides
with the old frame house

on an American street, the garden of hawthorn, bougainvillea, amaryllis,
the red maple, and her life.

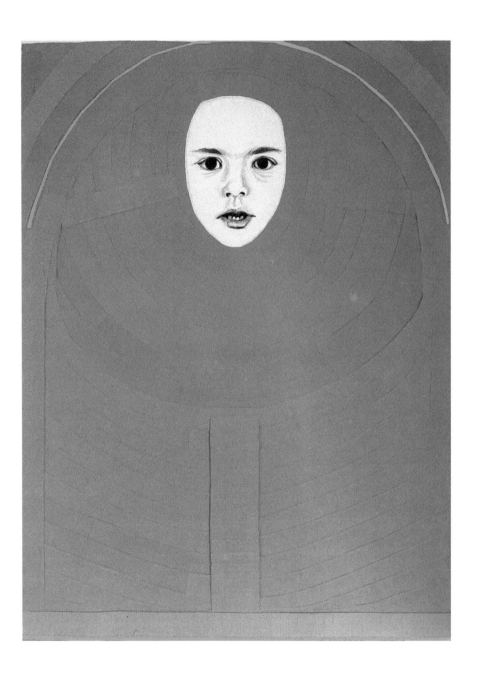

MENDING PAJAMAS

With her sewing basket open, sprawling,
she searches for thread to match these old silk pajamas,
their slick fabric covered with tiny birds of paradise.

Most of the thread is rotten, will not hold the seams
that pull, split with age, what her adult children call *vintage*.
She doesn't care. This stitching and restitching

is the work of prayer. An ancient call to the body to remake itself
as mind. She works the aqua thread into the nearly invisible
needle's eye, pulls it gently until she sees it pass through.

This, a morning's victory, she finishes her mending,
packs her basket away, waits for the miniscule whirring
at her window, hummingbirds among the blue-violet salvia.

DEDICATION & ACKNOWLEDGMENTS

This poem cycle has been crafted as a conversation with two beloved women poets whose work and friendship I have valued for many years, Carolyn Forché and Ewa Lipska. I am grateful to Ewa for her *Droga pani Schubert (Dear Ms. Schubert)* poems—the inspiration for Mrs. Schmetterling—and for her patience with my slow translation of her work into English. I am grateful to Carolyn for her exquisite poems and for long walks in Paris and in the forest of my imagination.

My deep thanks also to Polish poet Zbigniew Herbert, for his poem cycle *Pan Cogito/Mr. Cogito* (Trans. John and Bogdana Carpenter, Ecco Press, 1993), and to my dear friends and mentors, Edward Hirsch and Adam Zagajewski, for their poems and essays, and for introducing me to Polish poetry. And to beloved Adam, for welcoming me to his beautiful city of Kraków many years ago.

Warmest thanks to visual artist Sarah Fisher for granting me permission to use her image, "Stain – Self Portrait," as the cover art for this book, and to include additional images from the "Stain" cycle as companion pieces to the poems.

My sincerest thanks to all at Arrowsmith Press—in particular, Askold Melnyczuk for his faith in the Mrs. Schmetterling poems and his willingness to publish them, and Ezra Fox for his conception of the book's beautiful design. I am enormously grateful for the generous collaborative spirit that informs Askold's and Ezra's work with the authors whose work they steward into print.

I wish to express my gratitude to the editors of publications in which the following Mrs. Schmetterling poems have appeared:

"Mrs. Schmetterling Kneels in a Garden," "City that Ripens on the Tree of the World," "Sorites and Sand," "Mrs. Schmetterling Thinks of Her Heart," "Mrs. Schmetterling Considers the Beautiful," and "In the Balance of Final Things" appeared in *City That Ripens on the Tree of the World* (chapbook), Calypso Editions, 2013 and the collection *Luminous Other*, Ashland Poetry Press, 2013.

"What Mrs. Schmetterling Wants" ("Czego pragnie pani Schmetterling") appeared in Polish translation by Ewa Elżbieta Nowakowska in Rzeszów, Poland's literary journal *Fraza*, 2014.

"Mrs. Schmetterling Buries Her Mother," "Oak Cottage," "Mending Pajamas," and "Limbo at the Edge of an Abyss" appeared in *The High Window*, Issue 21, Spring 2021, with special thanks to editor David Cooke.

Love and thanks to poet Martha Serpas, the dear friend for whom the poem "Mending Pajamas" was written, and to my husband Tony Davidson, always.

These poems are also dedicated to my daughter, Chelsea Davidson Lindquist, and my daughter-in-law, Jamie Lynn Wise, with admiration for their strength as women—and with love.

NOTES

TITLE:

Schmetterling is the German word for "butterfly." It signifies the Dadaist notion of beauty as accident, developed in resistance to the reasoned, strategic atrocities of World War I. (*Schmetterling* is also the name given to the experimental German antiaircraft missile, the Henschel Hs 117, a radio-guided surface-to-air missile project developed near the close of World War II. The formal deployment planned for March 1945 never occurred.)

MRS. SCHMETTERLING KNEELS IN A GARDEN:

The name *Judith* is the Hebrew word for "praised" or "Jewess." The Book of Judith is a deuterocanonical text excluded from the Hebrew canon, and relegated to the apocrypha by Protestants. The story of Judith is that of a beautiful, courageous widow who never remarries and saves the Israelites from the Assyrians by gaining the trust of, and decapitating, the Assyrian general, Holofernes.

MRS. SCHMETTERLING THINKS OF HER HEART:

Lwów, founded in 1256 C.E., remained a part of Polish territory through much of the early twentieth century. The city was seized by the Soviets in 1939 and renamed Lvov. From 1941 to 1944 the city was occupied by the Nazis who created the Lvov (or Lemberg) Ghetto, housing about 120,000 Jews nearly all of whom were exterminated. Simon Wiesenthal, famous Nazi hunter and dear friend of Ewa Lipska, was one of the few who survived. In 1945 Lvov became part of the Ukraine under Soviet rule, and was renamed Lviv in 1991 when the Ukraine achieved independence from the USSR.

City that Ripens on the Tree of the World:
Krupnicza Street and Mickiewicz Avenue are located in Kraków, Poland. Adam Mickiewicz was a Polish Romantic poet famous for his epic, *Pan Tadeusz*, celebrating Polish nationalism. *Krupnik* (from which the name *Krupnicza* derives) refers in Polish to the "barley" used in a Polish soup or kasha, as well as the grain spirits combined with honey to make a mead-like alcoholic beverage.

Sorites and Sand:
Siostry means "sister" in Polish. *Sorites* refers to a sequence of linked syllogisms in logic, the conclusion of each syllogism becoming the major premise of the next syllogism. The term derives from the Greek word for "heap" and refers to the logical paradox that uses as its central metaphor a heap of sand to ask the question: "If a heap is reduced by a single grain of sand at a time, at what exact point does it cease to be considered a heap?"

Chestnut Trees:
The season referred to in the poem is both that of late spring (May when chestnuts bloom in Poland), and of the weeklong period of *matura* during which all Polish secondary school students must take a matriculation or exit exam to determine whether they may proceed to apply to a university or other institution of higher education and pursue postsecondary study. The *Planty*, one of Kraków's largest city parks, surrounds the Stare Miasto (*Old Town*) where the medieval city walls stood until the early 19th century, and is bordered by a pathway of lovely trees, most of which are chestnuts.

Mrs. Schmetterling Thinks of Returning to the City Where She Was Born:
This poem takes its title from Zbigniew Herbert's "Mr. Cogito Thinks of Returning to the City Where He Was Born" translated from the Polish by John and Bogdana Carpenter.

LIST OF ARTWORKS BY SARAH FISHER

COVER: **Stain — Self Portrait** (2018)
Oil, dry cleaning identification stickers and magnets on Arches paper
71 x 51 inches
Collection of Dennis Pow-Sang

PAGE 15: **Fold** (2019)
Oil and dry cleaning identification stickers on canvas
60 x 48 inches

PAGE 18: **Repair** (2020)
Oil, graphite, correction fluid, and dry cleaning identification stickers on Arches paper
71 x 51 inches

PAGE 21: **The Cold Place** (2019)
Oil, graphite and dry cleaning identification stickers on Arches paper
71 x 51 inches

PAGE 22: **Untitled** (2020)
Oil and dry cleaning identification stickers on Arches paper
30 x 22 inches

PAGE 25: **Repair — Self Portrait** (2018)
Linocut, oil markers and dry cleaning identification stickers on Arches paper
30 x 22 inches

Houston's second Poet Laureate (2015–2017), Robin Davidson is the author of two poetry chapbooks, *Kneeling in the Dojo* and *City that Ripens on the Tree of the World*, and the full collection, *Luminous Other*, recipient of the Ashland Poetry Press 2012 Richard Snyder Memorial Publication Prize. The recipient of Fulbright and NEA awards, she is co-translator with Ewa Elżbieta Nowakowska of two volumes of Ewa Lipska's poems from the Polish, *The New Century* and *Dear Ms. Schubert* (Princeton University Press, 2021). She was inducted into the Texas Institute of Letters in 2019, and teaches literature and creative writing as professor emeritus of English for the University of Houston-Downtown.

photo by Pin Lim

Sarah Fisher records the human need to be authentically seen in paintings, drawings and mixed-media works. She has exhibited across the state of Texas, including solo exhibitions at LHUCA (2021) in Lubbock and at Front Gallery (2019) and Art Palace Gallery (2017) in Houston. Fisher's mixed media work featured prominently in *Found/Loaded*, a joint exhibition with Rachel Anderson at Stephen F. Austin State University's Cole Art Center in 2021. A 1986 graduate of the University of Notre Dame, she completed the BLOCK Advanced Studio Program at The Museum of Fine Arts Houston's Glassell School in 2018. Fisher lives and works in Houston, Texas.

ARROWSMITH is named after the late William Arrowsmith, a renowned classics scholar, literary and film critic. General editor of thirty-three volumes of *The Greek Tragedy in New Translations*, he was also a brilliant translator of Eugenio Montale, Cesare Pavese, and others. Arrowsmith, who taught for years in Boston University's University Professors Program, championed not only the classics and the finest in contemporary literature, he was also passionate about the importance of recognizing the translator's role in bringing the original work to life in a new language.

Like the arrowsmith who turns his arrows straight and true,
a wise person makes his character straight and true.

— Buddha

Books by

ARROWSMITH

PRESS

Girls by Oksana Zabuzhko

Bula Matari/Smasher of Rocks by Tom Sleigh

This Carrying Life by Maureen McLane

Cries of Animal Dying by Lawrence Ferlinghetti

Animals in Wartime by Matiop Wal

Divided Mind by George Scialabba

The Jinn by Amira El-Zein

Bergstein edited by Askold Melnyczuk

Arrow Breaking Apart by Jason Shinder

Beyond Alchemy by Daniel Berrigan

Conscience, Consequence: Reflections on Father Daniel Berrigan edited by Askold Melnyczuk

Ric's Progress by Donald Hall

Return To The Sea by Etnairis Rivera

The Kingdom of His Will by Catherine Parnell

Eight Notes from the Blue Angel by Marjana Savka

Fifty-Two by Melissa Green

Music In—And On—The Air by Lloyd Schwartz

Magpiety by Melissa Green

Reality Hunger by William Pierce

Soundings: On The Poetry of Melissa Green edited by Sumita Chakraborty

The Corny Toys by Thomas Sayers Ellis

Black Ops by Martin Edmunds

Museum of Silence by Romeo Oriogun

City of Water by Mitch Manning

Passeggiate by Judith Baumel

Persephone Blues by Oksana Lutsyshyna

The Uncollected Delmore Schwartz edited by Ben Mazer

The Light Outside by George Kovach

The Blood of San Gennaro by Scott Harney edited by Megan Marshall

No Sign by Peter Balakian

Firebird by Kythe Heller

The Selected Poems of Oksana Zabuzhko edited by Askold Melnyczuk

The Age of Waiting by Douglas J. Penick

Manimal Woe by Fanny Howe

Crank Shaped Notes by Thomas Sayers Ellis

The Land of Mild Light by Rafael Cadenas edited by Nidia Hernández

The Silence of Your Name by Alexandra Marshall

Flame in a Stable by Martin Edmunds

CPSIA information can be obtained
at www.ICGtesting.com
Printed in the USA
BVHW022243281121
622744BV00002B/20